1st Edition

Baroque Medusa

Photographer: TB

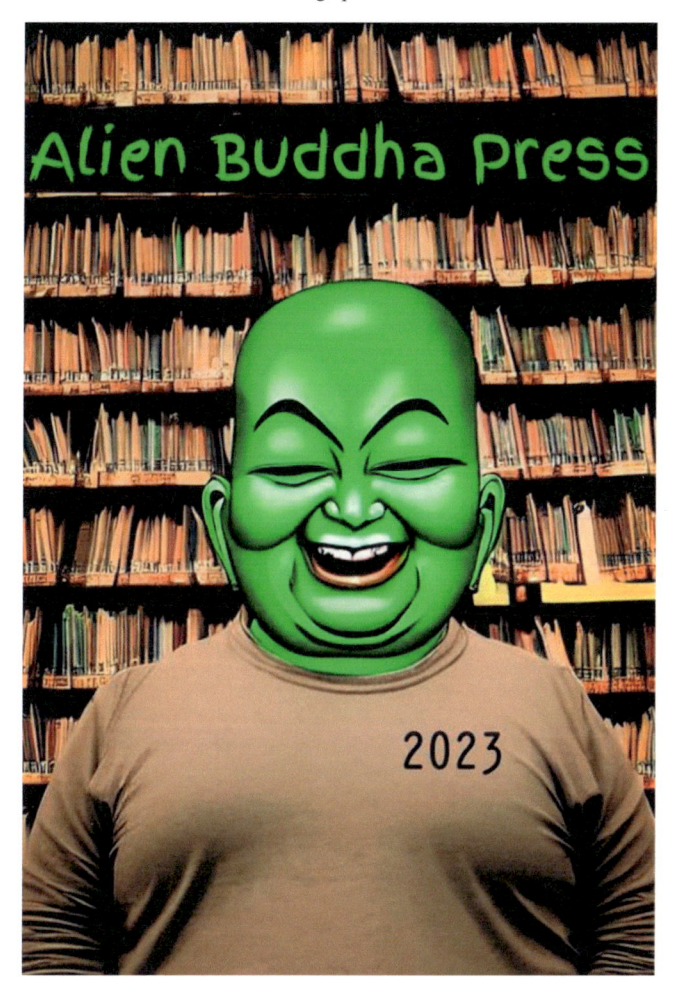

abuddhapress@yahoo.com

ISBN: 979-8859961825

Alien Buddha Press 2023

©™®

Baroque Medusa 2023

Table of Contents

1. Cherry
2. 3rd Base
3. User Friendly
4. Subscribers
5. Attention
6. International
7. Fixate & Titillate
8. Descent
9. New Money

Cherry

The halo above Alexandrite
Anointed by those closest
Heavy from the wear
The fatigue at times
Leaves her lethargic

Not one to break character
Walks upright by day
The halo to remain
Dots all I's
Crosses all T's

Tonight, the halo dims its light

Phone propped on the counter
Recording her stages of undress
Shyness begins to dissipate

Tonight, is the night

Stepping into shower
Her halo cleansed anew
Sets it out to dry

Tonight, the fawn takes flight

Curious thoughts persist
Fresh out the shower
Combing her wet, jet-black, hair
Reaching for her phone
Watching the replay
A smirk

Tonight, no feelings of contrite

Phone back on counter
Presses record once more
Applying moisturizer
From head to toe
She slows it down
At her crotch

Tonight, she is tight

Index & middle fingers
Casually enter her
Gets into a rhythm with her left
Picks up her phone with the right

Tonight, she will reach new heights

Deep eye contact
Selfie mode

Release
A deep moan
As she licks her screen
Halo exchanged for horns

Tonight, this is one for the bytes

3rd Base

Halo on
Signals guilt
Ashamed of last night's actions
Nauseated
Phone gallery proclaiming sin

Today, signs of dismay

Sits in class
With thoughts of unease
Her halo shines again
With acts of godliness
She graces others
Little do they know

Today, she will no longer decay

As she walks the halls
Reminders of last night
Creep into her mind
Devil back on her shoulder
Temptation calls her name
A L E X A N D R I T E

Today, she no longer portrays

Phone waiting
To be touched
She enters the lady's room
Phone now in hand
Angel sprouts horns

Today, she cuts the horseplay

Her guilt
A double-edged sword
A turn on
To sin more
To stimulate more
To penetrate more

Today, she makes headway

Entering the stall
Pressing record
Arousal
Finding pleasure
In herself once more

Today, it's her way

Deep into selfie mode
Halo takes a tumble
Shatters upon the floor
Innocent no more
Anger now rushes through
Veins a bright purple

Today, she no longer stays

Climax approaching
No halo in sight
Silently moaning in delight

Today, she revels in gainsay

Satisfaction written
All over her face
Her moistened fingers
Now to her lips
Swiping left then right
Insertion into mouth
As she casually smirks
Licks them clean

Today, she gives way

One more look
Into selfie mode
Taking her now

Clean fingers
Swipes them across
Soul comes through her phone
"You can have more @ $10/month"

Today, she debuts on her Broadway

Phone returned to bag
The fallen angel
Tosses shattered halo
Into the public toilet
Gurgle of the water
Sends it to the abyss
Bye, Bitch

Today, her way or the highway

User Friendly

The bathroom
Any bathroom
Brings delight
Devoid of those who birthed
Her now non-existent crown

The bathroom, her playground

In front of her
Bathroom vanity
Is where she longs to be
Can stare deep within
To bare her soul

The bathroom, her get down

Today is different
Fawn takes the leap
Waiting impatiently
For the download to complete

The bathroom, she must simmer down

"Sign up for Only Fans"
On her phone screen
Creating her profile
Brings sensations
Stirs excitement

The bathroom, jumping up & down

Toggles back
Presses record
Lifting her skirt
Right hand slides
Panty to the side
The fawn in heat
Servicing herself

The bathroom, her hunting ground

There she is
Alexandrite pulsates
Alexandrite convulses
Her rhythm hypnotizing

Aglow like the Full Moon

The bathroom, touchdown

Born for the camera
Au Naturale
Blows a kiss
"See you on the other side"

The bathroom, spellbound

Bio complete
Ready to be a star
Draws herself a bath
Scent of lavender
Drifts through
Her favorite room

The bathroom, her private compound

Slowly sitting down
Submerges below
Complete silence
Alone in her thoughts

The bathroom, time to crack down

Silence no more
Notifications galore
Subscriber after subscriber

The bathroom, her new inbound

From fawn to superstar
"Off to the races"
Superstar celebrates
Vibrator set to high

The bathroom, she is now renowned

Reaching new heights
All on her own
She submerges herself
Beneath warm bathwater
Once more
"This is just the beginning"

The bathroom, never to live down

Subscribers

Ding, to the third degree
Notification after notification
Vixen never imagined

After all, pleasure herself, always a must

Dollar signs galore
All she wants is
To service herself
Watch over & over
Each replay triggers
Another round of
SATISFACTION

After all, pleasure herself, or combust

Each round
Took her to new heights
Each notification
Needs now insurmountable
THIRST

After all, pleasure herself, a wanderlust

Notification alerts
New erogenous zone
Each new pic
Each new video
Brings her new
Avenues

After all, pleasure herself, constructive trust

Alexandrite
Ready to mount
Bring in the dough

After all, pleasure herself, now an investment trust

Clitoris rock hard

Ready for blast off
"Take me home, Daddy"
PAY ME

After all, pleasure herself, also a charitable trust

Her fingers
Her best friends
Her subscriber's addiction
Anxiously await
To watch her
GLOW

After all, pleasure herself, NOT a discretionary trust

In her ~~bathroom~~ Escape Room
Reads her reviews
Thumb up
No dislikes

After all, pleasure herself, the new living trust

Escape Room
Repainted
With her voracious, insatiable moans
Mirrors steamed
Presses record
Taking herself to new heights

After all, pleasure herself, angel dust

"I'ma make you my bitch"
Licks her screen – her "signature"
Swipes her dripping fingers across the screen
"~~PAY ME~~ INSERT YOURSELF: here"

After all, pleasure herself, no breach of trust

Her moans
Deeper in base

Erect fingers tired
Her vaj
Slippery wet
She loves to love
Herself
More than anything

After all, pleasure herself, equivalent of gold dust

Self-satisfaction > everything
BUT THOSE DOLLAR IGN
Clit engorged
Ready to go
AGAIN
Needing release
AGAIN
Alexandrite turns the camera off

After all, pleasure herself, always stardust

Privacy for new heights
Not shareable
This is her time
To revel
In her own love
To glow
Her aura
Impenetrable
LICKS FINGERS
One last time
For the night

After all, pleasure herself, self-entrust

"This one was for me, only"

After all, pleasure herself, her one true lust

Attention

Auto-deposits roll in
Broadway playwright
Turned Only Fans
Highest rank phenom
Millionaire in the making

Alexandrite, the salacious

NC-17 phone gallery
All she wants
Find new ways
To bring herself to
Satisfaction

Alexandrite, the ostentatious

Microdosing bleeds
Into addiction
Throb of her vaj
Constant
Wallet seeking more
Constant
New subscribers
Constant
New explorations
Constant
Looking for a mate
Constant
Or two
Constant
To service her
$$$$$

Alexandrite, the flirtatious

Ad read:
Service me
Top me off
Suck me
Let my lips

Rain all over your
Red lipstick
All for the camera
$$$$$

Alexandrite, the bodacious

International

Influx of new funds
Leads to new pursuits
Satisfying herself
In new Escape Rooms

Take the show on the road, Millionaire will

Alexandrite arrives
Saunters up to her private jet
Main cabin all to herself
Door locked
Awaiting take-off
Engine roars
Propellers pulsate
Main cabin's constant buzz
Illuminates her need
TO GET OFF

Take the show on the road, Millionaire's new bank bill

Phone propped
Red button pressed
Only Fans highest rank
Slithers to and fro
Pupils dilate
Sugar Walls wrapped around
Index & middle fingers
TIGHT
WET
Glazed sugar-coated delight
Sweetness now to her lips
Natures candy in the limelight

Take the show on the road, Millionaire lives for the thrill

Ready for takeoff
She slows it down
Wants to
CLIMAX OUT LOUD
Yet

IN SECRECY

Take the show on the road, Millionaire must fulfill

Taxying down the runway
Private jet ramps up
Picks up her phone
Lowers it to her
Sugar Shack
Intimacy redefined
Moistness fogs
The lens

Take the show on the road, Millionaire's new chill

Legs wide open
Index & Middle
Slide on in
For it is
Their home
Loud rumbling of the jet
Speed faster & faster
She plays catch up
Moaning in ecstasy
Rock-a-bye baby
Virginal white leather seat
Now anointed with Starlet's
SUGAR FROSTING

Take the show on the road, Millionaire's in-air playbill

They take off
They stabilize
In unison
Jet now horizontal
As is our Millionaire
First show: Uploaded
Next stop: Worldwide

Take the show on the road, read Millionaire's handbill

Fixate & Titillate

Miami
New York
Florence
Amsterdam
Frivolity to some
Highest rank is
Living out loud

Come and put your name on it

Non-stop tour
One big Escape Room
Many a day and night
Pleasuring herself
New inspiration at
Every turn
New ways to
GET OFF

The scenery, lit

Miami, Florence, Amsterdam
Starlet attracted her muses
Camera devoured each session
Starlet coming all over
Deafening those within earshot
With her insatiable thirst
Glaze the cities with her
SUGAR FROSTING

They all must submit

New York
Starlet played the intimate card
Locked in her penthouse suite
Bell hop assisted in her quest
Free of phone in-hand

Starlet's makeshift cockpit

Hired help now camera man
Filming the starlet
From head to toe
Sheets and counter tops
Drenched in Starlet's
SUGAR FROSTING

Hurry up, lickety split

Starlet turns it up
Newly minted camera man
Turned Starlet's NY muse

Don't throw a fit

Camera on counter
Starlet's
SUGAR-SOAKED FINGERS
To NY Muse's lips
He exhales
Her fingers now being
SUCKED

NY Muse must commit

Camera Man turned muse
Places Starlet at the foot
Of her king size bed
Removing her skirt
Kneeling in front
HER LEGS AGAPE
Goes for the kill

The two, now tightly knit

In search of
MORE SUGAR
His hunger supersedes
Starlet's moaning
Massaging his head

Gets into rhythm
CULMINATING
His tongue her new
CONQUEST

One for the books, Holy Writ

Eye on the lens
RIDES
Muse's mouth
HARD
Glazed sugar
His new mask

Both reach a new orbit

Locked in
Muse removes trousers
Erect cock throbbing
Starlet zones in
Purses lips
TIP OFF

Starlet, not a hypocrite

Combustion
Exchange of each of their
SUGAR
All over each of their
FACE
MMM, de$$ert

The two, now close-knit

Descent

A recognized name
Across all platforms
International starlet
Her Sugar Shack
Her Sugar Walls
Her sugar-glazed lips

Taste of sweet success

Starlet, a sought-after commodity

Each day yields
The same content
Various poses
Different angles
Influx of new subscribers
Screeching halt

Starlet, a fading novelty

Alexandrite replaced
By the newest
Only Fans member

Starlet, now a monotony

Quick to rise
Faster to fall
Escape Room
Now tomb

Starlet starts a new odyssey

New Money

Second ranked
Light bulb epiphany
Starlet DM's Top Rank
"Escape Room?"

Starlet begins her second act

Join, they did
1st and 2nd place, now one
Alexandrite's Escape Room

Second act, far from abstract

Not one, but two
Phones
Recording their tryst
Arousal of senses
Stimulation of nerve endings
Births twitching
Hips gyrating
Top Rank's moan of
Approval
Ecsta$y to both

Second act renamed, Barebacked

Top Ranked
Brings our Starlet
Up for air
Their lips softly touch
Sharing Top Rank's sugar
Sets each soul on fire
GLOSSED LIPS
GLAZED TULIPS
HARD CLITS

Second act, a new pact

Taking turns
Brought a new dimension
Enthralled with each other
Chemistry translates into
Thirst
Lust
Fascination
Obsession

Infatuation
The need to satisfy
The others request

Second act, sugar-packed

Both tied
1st place
New subscribers
New auto deposits
Escape Room turned
Sugar Shack sanctuary
$$$$$

Second act, their new pact

Bio

The mind of Baroque Medusa holds many thoughts attached to vivid colors and graphic imagery. While many have dismissed the author as profane or explicit, Medusa refutes such claims.

"My thoughts have always been of a decadent, salacious, nature. They are beautiful creations, not provocations. Humans are primal. We live and breathe lust and desire. It's part of our DNA."

Made in the USA
Columbia, SC
29 October 2023